16 Ma

Another year, a little better than the last, or is it just me growing old? No, well done and thank you

All my love

Dad
xxxxx

Published by Yorkshire Sculpture Park

ISBN   1 871480 63 9

Photography: Jonty Wilde
Book design: Sarah Coulson
Printed in UK by Derek Hattersley & Son, Barnsley
Audio recording: Smallcog

The Song of Wandering Aengus is reproduced with the
permission of A.P. Watt Ltd on behalf of Gráinne Yeats.
The Road Not Taken, published in *Mountain Interval*, 1916,
by Henry Holt.

Produced with the support of:

CALOUSTE
GULBENKIAN
FOUNDATION

Simon Armitage
The Twilight Readings

YSP Yorkshire Sculpture Park

Foreword
Simon Armitage

I gave my first ever poetry reading at Bretton Hall College, with three other poets from a local writers' workshop. I'm guessing it was 1987. We hadn't really been invited and we certainly weren't being paid: a space was available and we decided to occupy it. We hand-wrote a flyer for the event, ran off a couple of dozen copies and stuck them in shop windows around Kirklees. The venue was the clapped-out student union – a converted stable or kennel block, I think. As I recall, the first half of the show consisted of a one-woman "devised performance piece" on the subject of family dysfunction and marital disharmony, and the second half consisted of the three of us reading to an audience made up entirely of ourselves. There may have been six or seven other bodies leaning on the bar at the back, but for them the poetry was only a distraction to their drinking. And vice versa. Afterwards we shuffled outside, and against the dwindling crimson light of a summer evening, the silhouettes of various statues and sculptures became apparent against the horizon, like big game in a safari park, stirring in the dusk. I was staggered that the pieces were simply left there overnight, and not wheeled away into some enormous hangar and covered with oilcloth. It seemed so blatant, so brazen, and so brave.

Despite the farce and failure of the reading, that inauspicious occasion marked the beginning of a relationship with the Sculpture Park which has now lasted two decades and which has grown stronger and more important over time. The point, I think, is that even in its early years, YSP represented a confident form of self-expression, an unembarrassed public airing of creative endeavour on a large, external scale, which as a poet I found daring and inspiring. Poetry can be a shy little thing. Poets tend to conduct their business in private. Poems, if they are fortunate enough to be published, tend to be read in silence before being buried alive within the covers of a book, sometimes never to see the light of day again. YSP, on the other hand, has always been about getting art into the public domain, with people walking amongst it, picnicking beneath it, and sometimes (not always to the delight of the staff) clambering all over it. In fact the very concept of a sculpture park seems to fly in the face of more purist notions of art, and maybe YSP's very existence can be thought of as part of a long, northern tradition of non-conformism and dissent. Added to this, I sense amongst the community of its staff a kind of infectious exhilaration and excitement – as if they are making the whole thing up as they go along. Opportunities are seized, obstacles are overcome, notions are acted upon, day-dreams are transmuted into realities. YSP might have endured and evolved to the point where it can now be considered part of the establishment, but its original values persist, and the spirit of adventure continues. If YSP encouraged me to think more about getting my own work into the public arena, I've absorbed (and sometimes stolen) many other creative ideologies from within its boundaries, most recently the idea that art need not seek to be permanent and eternal. Andy Goldsworthy's work is especially relevant to this thought. His snowballs melt, his dam-walls burst open, his pools of dandelion heads are swept away by the current, his expelled saliva evaporates, and livestock lumber indifferently through and across his creations. Even with his recent exhibition at YSP, where less delicate and more resolute structures have come into being, a sense of obsolescence – even mortality – still pervades. At an imperceptible level the clay cracks, the wood rots, the leaf-stems wither, the dung perishes, the blood decays. Precariousness is everywhere: even the sturdy walls and stone arches, held together by their own weight, owe everything to the complex gravitational balance of the planets and stars in which they hang.

In its thirtieth anniversary year, YSP offered me a working residency. In a sense they were only making formal what had been taking place for many years – as if they had seen me mooching about in the grounds for too long and had finally decided to invite me in for a cup of tea. I asked to be described as visiting artist rather than a visiting poet or writer, because I imagined working with the physicality of language – seeing poetry as a fashioned and fabricated substance, sculpted from words. I had grand notions about growing poems in fields of corn, or erecting a poetic shrine to the environment, or studding the old gallops along the edge of the lake with poems engraved onto horseshoes. I even had a brainstorm about hanging hundreds of shoes by their laces from a dead tree – I kept that one to myself. In the end, though, and in the nick of time, I realised I should be bringing my own thing to YSP, not trying to emulate the practice of others. And my own thing is writing and reading – reacting and responding with written and spoken language. YSP, as well as being an unlimited source of poetic subject matter, also contains dozens of accidental but convenient and atmospheric venues for a poetry reading. I decided on a series of readings, all to take place in the final week of September in the fading light of summer and in the failing light of day. The venues for these Twilight Readings included the Camellia House, the Deer Shelter Skyspace, the Underground Gallery, and the little known Greek temple in the nature reserve (advertised as 'The Mystery Location'). As a celebratory conclusion, the final reading would take place at the Longside Gallery. I did propose a sixth venue at one stage, the idea being to read from within the walled circle of Goldsworthy's Outclosure, with the audience being positioned around the external circumference. But I ditched the notion in the end. As well as being problematic on all kinds of practical levels, it bordered on a kind of theatricality that would have turned a poetry reading into a stunt. Throw a strong wind and an autumn gale into the equation, and the stunt could quite easily have become a fiasco.

Two types of poems emerged. The first were anecdotal, prose-looking things, like little stories. I was interested in taking one small detail from within the venue, such as a colour, or shape, or object, or even a word, and letting the narrative of the poem grow from it, like an undisturbed daydream. The second were translations from the Wakefield Mystery Plays, the cycle of mediaeval religious pageants which are closely associated with the region and which have been performed at Bretton College on a number of occasions. In the Middle Ages the Mystery Plays were presented by different local guilds on makeshift stages or floats, and in that sense fitted in well with my programme of changing locations and improvised venues. I chose five dramatic monologues, each one having some relationship with the intended setting, and translated them from the original Middle English into contemporary (but still colloquial) verse.

I asked that the readings should not be filmed. I wanted these to be intimate and unique events, entirely for the benefit of those who attended (in the case of the Deer Shelter Skyspace the numbers had to be restricted to as few as twenty-five, and not a great deal more in some of the other locations). But they were recorded, and at the end of the week the sound engineer reflected back to me how many of the poems had been about death. Perhaps this is inevitable with bible stories, with people always meeting their maker or marching towards the grave (and in the case of Lazarus, returning from it). As for the prose poems, I can only think that their darkness derives from the art itself, that transience in Goldsworthy's work mentioned earlier, which at times goes further than mere impermanence and exhibits, to my way of thinking, a kind of death-in-life quality (to borrow a Ted Hughes phrase). Because for all that his work connects with the living planet, there is a funereal aspect also, be it in the urns or tombs of the sandstone domes, the chthonic chambers of the Clay Room (not to mention the human hair and its atrocious associations), the burial mound or unlit pyre of the Wood Room, the skeletal Hanging Trees in their grave-shaped ossuaries, or the decomposing shroud of the Leaf Stalk Room. Even his Shadow Stone Fold seems to me to be a shrine to a way of life that teeters on the brink of extinction. Goldsworthy's creations and structures are never triumphant monuments to posterity. For all they celebrate the natural world, with its glorious workings and magnificent components, they also commemorate our brief existence within it. Most of my YSP poems, I think, have been written in some of the darker shadows cast by his work.

So my contribution to YSP's thirtieth anniversary year has not been one of material products but one of happenings and events. Site-specific readings, including site-specific poems, delivered in the mysterious light of dusk. Events which I hope will live on in the memory of those present, long after the breath which launched them has long evaporated into the night.

The Road Not Taken

Two roads diverged in a yellow wood,
And sorry I could not travel both
And be one traveler, long I stood
And looked down one as far as I could
To where it bent in the undergrowth;

Then took the other, as just as fair,
And having perhaps the better claim,
Because it was grassy and wanted wear;
Though as for that the passing there
Had worn them really about the same,

And both that morning equally lay
In leaves no step had trodden black.
Oh, I kept the first for another day!
Yet knowing how way leads on to way,
I doubted if I should ever come back.

I shall be telling this with a sigh
Somewhere ages and ages hence:
Two roads diverged in a wood, and I —
I took the one less traveled by,
And that has made all the difference.

Robert Frost

Camellia House
Sunday 23 September 2007

My Camellias

I've been writing a lot of poems recently about my camellias, but my tutor isn't impressed. Even though he hasn't said as much, it's clear that as far as he's concerned, my camellias don't *cut much ice*. He wants me to dress my camellias with tinsel and bells and flashing lights, or stick them on a float and drive them through town at the head of the May Day Parade. "Tell me one interesting fact about your camellias," he says, so I tell him about the time I lost a camellia down the plughole in a Bournemouth guesthouse and had to fish it back with a tooth-pick on a length of dental floss. He says, "Er, that's not really what I had in mind, Henry." Basically he'd prefer my camellias to die in a fire, or be ritually amputated in a civil war. Then he shows me a prize-winning poem (one of his own, in fact) about a pair of camellias, twins in fact, who were swapped at birth by a childless midwife, and who grew up quite differently, one in the bosom of the Saudi Royal Family, the other beneath the "jackboot of poverty," and who met in later life only to discover the absolute symmetry of their colours and petal structures. He wants me to lock one of my camellias in a coal cellar until it comes of age then take it outside and reverse over it with the ride-on lawnmower, or auction a camellia in the global marketplace, or film it brazenly copulating in a busy street, or scream the details of my camellias into the rabbit hole of the cosmos hoping to bend the ear of creation itself. I tell him I once swallowed a camellia without water on an empty stomach, but he isn't listening anymore. He's quoting some chap who went at his camellia with a pair of pinking-shears. He's talking about such-and-such a poet who threw her camellia in front of the queen's carriage, or about camellias which were beaten senseless by plain-clothed officers then rendered down into potting compost or wallpaper paste or lined up against the wall on prime-time national TV. And when I plead with him that no matter how small and pitiful my own camellias might seem to him, to me they are everything, he looks at me with a wounding expression, one which suggests that in his all-seeing, all-knowing eyes I am little more than a complete and undisguised and irreversible dandelion.

Mind from my path for here come I,
the most detested far and wide,
at full pelt through the countryside
and into town.
Yes, into town now come have I
down from the mount of Calvary
where Christ does dangle, hanging high,
I swear you by my crown.

At Calvary where hanged he was
I spat my sputum in his face,
and there it shone like crystal glass
so seemly to my sight.
Fair play, then as a further thing
at him I laughed, and in my loathing
lightened him of all his clothing,
as of right.

And when his clothes were fully off,
Lord how we cheered and laughed
and with a briar crowned that scruff
as though he were a king.
Then in due course
full curiously I thought
to wrap his corpse
in faith for him to swing.

But to my God I make a vow,
here have I brought this clothing now
to try the truth before your law
and in your sight.
Between me and my fellows two
these garments two of us must lose;
Sir Pontius Pilate thou must choose,
this very night.

For whosoever keeps these clothes
will want for nothing where he goes,
and luck its wind will to him blow
if he them wears.
So now my comrades of renown
let devilment in us abound
and in our gang we'll gather round
and gossip of this gear.

Second Torturer

Stand back yourselves from me at once
and let me through this crowd advance,
for I shall bop him on the bonce
who stands in my way.
Look, I will leap and I will skip
as if I were devoid of wit;
my kex I damn near did be-shit
for dread I came so late.

But now, by heavens, I am here
the most unloved, and that I swear,
that ye shall find most anywhere.
Spell pain my name beware!
I too at Calvary was this day,
Calvary where the Jew King lay,
and taught him a new game to play
which to me seemed fair.

The game we shared has some renown:
that he should lay his napper down
and then I cuffed him on his crown.
That game I thought was good.
We played until we had our fill
and then we led him up a hill
and there we wrought him with our will
and hung him on a rood.

But quite enough of all this chatter;
to the heart-meat of the matter
which brings me here at such a clatter:
this coat I wish I had.
For if this coat myself could keep
then I would skip and I would leap
and even fast from drink and meat
as if I were mad.

Third Torturer

Look out yourselves and mind your bones
for I come hurtling all at once
and damn near broke both bollock stones
so fast hurried I hither.
Not one thing pleases me better in life
than to murder a robber or hang a thief
and if here be any that give me grief
I shall them thrash together.

For this I promise, for my sins,
I am most hated of my kin
from this town to as far as Lynn.
Lo, my colleague torturers,
now will we fellow men
a new game with ourselves begin
the same coat one of us to win,
and our fates and futures.

Camellia House

William Pye
Shaun Pickard

Deer Shelter Skyspace
Tuesday 25 September 2007

from
The Second Shepherd's Play

First Shepherd

Lord, but this weather is cold and I am ill-equipped;
my fist is iced-curled so long have I kipped;
my legs they fold and my fingers are stripped;
it is not as I would, for I am all gripped
in sorrow.
In storms and tempest
now to east, now to west,
unhappy is him that never rests
this day or tomorrow.

We innocent shepherds who walk the moor
were ushered high-handedly out of the door;
no wonder, as it stands, that we be poor,
for the tilth of our land lies fallow as the floor.
I tell you then:
we are fleeced and rammed,
with taxes slammed,
and tamed by hand
by these gentlemen.

They rape us of rest – let Mary make them wary,
these pompous pests who make the plough tarry.
Some say it's for the best but we find contrary,
thus are farmhands oppressed: no hope do they carry
alive.
Thus hold they us under
and bring us to blunder.
It were great wonder
if ever should we thrive.

Should a man show a stylish sleeve or a brooch nowadays,
take care if you him grieve or dispute what he say;
dare no man deprive him of his powerful ways,
and yet no man believe one word that he says -
not one letter.
He gets his ill-gains
with big-headed claims,
and boasts he's maintained
by men even greater.

So up swans some swain who is peacock proud,
who must borrow my wain and also my plough,
and with no gainsaying I must grant him out loud
or I live in pain and anger and woe.
For by night and day
every hope he hankers
I must hand it over.
It better they hang us
than say to him Nay.

It does me good to walk on my own,
to make my talk of the world and to moan.
To my sheep will I stalk and listen alone
and keep watch from a balk or sit on a stone
some time soon.
Though if truth be,
I expect to see
dubious company
well before noon.

5pm

close gate

The Apprentice

So George has this theory: the first thing we ever steal, when we're young, is a symbol of what we become later in life, when we grow up. Example: when he was nine he stole a Mont Blanc fountain pen from a fancy gift shop in a hotel lobby – now he's an award winning novelist. We test the theory around the table and it seems to check out. Clint stole a bottle of cooking-sherry, now he owns a tapas bar. Kirsty's an investment banker and she stole money from her mother's purse. Tod took a Curly Wurly and he's morbidly obese. Claude says he never stole anything in his whole life, and he's an actor i.e. unemployed. Derek says, "But wait a second, I stole a blue Smurf on a polythene parachute," and Kirsty says, "So what more proof do we need, Derek?" Every third Saturday in the month I collect my son from his mother's house and we take off, sometimes to the dog-track, sometimes into the great outdoors. Last week we headed into the Western Range to spend a night under the stars and to get some quality time together, father and son. With nothing more than a worm, a paperclip and thread of cotton we caught a small, ugly-looking fish; I was all for tossing it back in the lake, but Isaac surprised me by slapping it dead on a flat stone, slitting its belly and washing out its guts in the stream. Then he cooked it over a fire of brushwood and dead leaves, and for all the thinness of its flesh and the annoying little needles of its bones, it made an honest meal. Later on, as it started dropping dark, we bedded down in an old deer shelter on the side of the hill. There was a hole in the roof. Sometimes the stars seemed as hard and as bright as nail-heads. A minute later they looked like their own timid reflections, cowering tremulously at the bottom of an ancient well of uncertain depth. Remembering George's theory, I said to Isaac, "So what do you think you'll be, when you grow up?" He was barely awake, but from somewhere in his sinking thoughts and with a drowsy voice he said, "I'm going to be an executioner." Now the hole in the roof was an ear, the ear of the universe, excessively interested in my response. I sat up, rummaged about in the bottom of the rucksack, struck a match, then said, "Hold on a minute, son, you're talking about taking a person's life. Why would you want to say a thing like that?" Without a flicker of reaction or even opening his eyes he said, "But I'm sure I could do it. Pull the hood over someone's head, squeeze the syringe, flick the switch, whatever. You know, if they'd done wrong. Now go to sleep, Dad."

Underground Gallery
Wednesday 26 September 2007

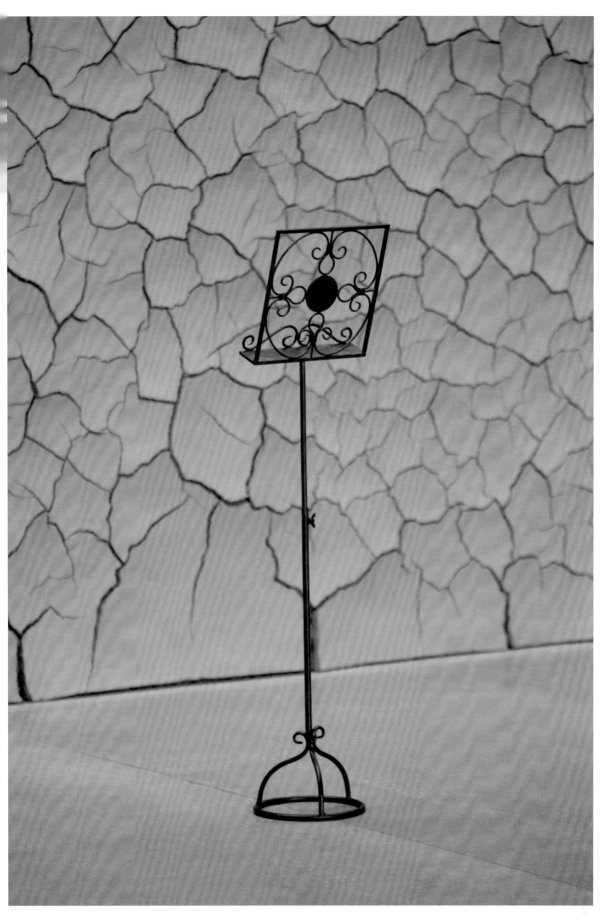

I'll Be There To Love And Comfort You

The couple next door were testing the structural fabric of the house with their difference of opinion. "I can't take much more of this," I said to Mimi, my wife. Right at that moment there was another almighty crash, as if every pan in the kitchen had clattered to the tiled floor. Mimi said, "Try and relax. Take one of your tablets." She brewed a pot of camomile tea and we retired to bed. But the pounding and caterwauling went on right into the small hours. I was dreaming that the mother-of-all asteroids was locked on a collision course with planet Earth, when unbelievably a fist came thumping through the bedroom wall just above the headboard. In the metallic light of the full moon I saw the bloody knuckles and a cobweb tattoo on the flap of skin between finger and thumb, before the fist withdrew. Mimi's face was powdered with dirt and dust, but she didn't wake. She looked like a dead mother pulled from the rubble of an earthquake after five days in a faraway country famous only for its paper kites. I peered through the hole in the wall. It was dark on the other side, with just occasional flashes of purple or green light, like those weird electrically-powered life-forms zipping around in the ocean depths. There was a rustling noise, like something stirring in a nest of straw, then a little voice, a voice no bigger than a sixpence, crying for help. Suddenly Mimi was right next to me. "It's her," she said. I said, "Don't be crazy, Mimi, she'd be twenty-four by now." "It's her I tell you. Get her back, do you hear me? GET HER BACK." I rolled up my pyjama sleeve and pushed my arm into the hole, first to my elbow, then as far as my shoulder and neck. The air beyond was clammy and damp, as if I'd reached into a nineteenth century London street in late November, fog rolling in up the river, a cough in a doorway. Mimi was out of her tiny mind by now. My right cheek and my ear were flat to the wall. Then slowly but slowly I opened my fist to the unknown. And out of the void, slowly but slowly it came: the pulsing starfish of a child's hand, swimming and swimming and coming to settle on my upturned palm.

from
Lazarus

Lazarus

Lord, that all things made from nought,
glory be to thee,
that such wonder here has wrought,
greater may none be.
When I was dead, dark hell I sought,
but thou, a guide to me,
raised me up and hence me brought.
Behold, as you may see.

There is none so bold on earth,
nor none of pride nor worth,
nor none so daring in his deeds
nor none so properly esteemed,
no sovereign, no soldier, no man-of-the-street,
that death can cheat.
Nor flesh, when it desires to feed,
but shall be worms' meat.

Your death is worms' cook.
I am your mirror – look.
Let myself be your book –
your lesson take from me.
And though from death you shirk and duck,
dead shall you all be.

To each so finely arrayed, death shall deliver its swipe,
and encase him in cold clay, be he king or knight,
and for all his piping and braid that were seemly in sight,
his flesh shall melt away, him and every type.
Then worms, taking bite,
shall gnaw day and night
at their lungs and their lights.
and their hearts eat asunder.
Thus both misters and masters from great heights
shall be brought under.

Beneath the earth you all shall cower and couch;
the roof of your hall your naked nose shall touch;
neither the great nor small before you will kneel nor crouch;
a sheet shall be your pall, and toads your jewels. Much
slime shall you wear,
fiends will you fear,
your flesh that was once fair
shall ruefully rot.
Instead of a stiff collar
tight bindings shall lag your throat.

Your glow that was rosy red shall pale to lily-like,
and be wan as lead, and stink like a dog got drowned in a dyke;
worms therein shall be bred as are bees in a hive,
and your eyes from your head shall the natterjacks drive.
So to pick at your food
come many uncommon beast,
and thus, from your flesh and blood,
shall be made a feast.

Mystery Location: Temple
Friday 28 September 2007

Joseph

Well, now, this is a wondrous thing.
Of it my mind should rest,
but in my breast my heart is sore
and all the longer more and more.
What should I do for best?

God's and mine she says it is,
but of my fatherhood resists.
She shows me shame, and yet
her villainy is not excused by me;
with her I will no longer be,
and rue the day we met.

And how we met you're soon to know:
men have their younger children go
to the temple to learn.
And so went she, until she grew more,
and than the other maidens knew more;
then bishops said to her:

"Mary it falls on thee to take
some young man here to make thy mate
as others have.
In this temple who wilt thou name?"
And she said none but God in heaven
would she love.

And would have no other that she saw.
They said she must, it was the law,
now being a woman.
To the temple they gathered old and young
and those of Judea's offspring sprung;
all were summoned.

Each was given a white-coloured wand,
and had us bear it in our hand,
to offer with good intent.
Then all men held their wands up high,
but I was old and stood aside,
knowing not what they meant.

They lacked one. Each and all, they chimed,
had offered wands, except for mine,
for I stood withdrawn.
Forward with wand they made me come,
and in my hand it fruited and bloomed.
Then said they all:

"Thou may be old, but a marvel it is
that your ordination is heaven's wish,
as the wand shows so surely.
It flourishes, and in flourishing states
that marriage to Mary the maid awaits."
Then was I sorry.

Sorry indeed to be this way caught,
so past my prime of youth I thought
of marriage never.
What use was I to her so young?
They said that I should hold my tongue,
and wed us together.

When she and I were joined as one
we and my maidens journeyed home,
who were kings' daughters,
and silk they worked at, everyone,
but she worked purple on its own,
and no other colours.

I left them in happy peace, no doubt,
and travelled the country thereabout
my trade to ply
and to earn the living that we should need.
And of Mary I prayed them take good heed
till home came I.

Nine months I was from Mary mild.
When I came home she was with child.
I said alas, for shame!
I asked the maids who had that done;
they said it was an angel come
while I was gone from home.

An angel-kind did with her stay
and no other male by night or day.
"Accept it, sir, be bold."
Thus they explained the matter fully
to clean excuse her of her folly
and taunt me for being old.

Could an angel this deed have brought about?
Such wild excuses help me nought,
no matter what miracles angels plan.
In truth, a heavenly thing is he,
and she is earthly: this may not be.
It is some other man.

Indeed I am wounded by her deed,
but this is how youth has always been,
full of wanton ways.
Young women desire to have their fun
not with aged man but fellow young.
Thus was it always.

But Mary and I played never the same.
Never as two did we play that game
nor ever came close.

As pure as crystal is my wife
and shall be all my living life,
the law decrees it so.
So of Mary's deed am I to blame?
Can any sage or prophet name
a cure for my woe?

And so, in truth, if it is done
that God in heaven's earthly son
she carries inside,
then clear as day it is that I
worthily never again can lie
her blessed body beside,

nor even in her company be.
To the wilderness then I will hurry me,
to what fate holds in store.
And no longer with Mary will I deal,
but silently off from her shall steal,
that meet shall we no more.

The Practical Way To Heaven

The opening of the new exhibition space at the Sculpture Farm had been a wonderful success. "Would all those visitors returning to London on the 3.18 from Wakefield Westgate please make their way to the main entrance from where the shuttle bus is about to depart," announced a nasally Maggie over the P.A. system. She'd been having trouble with her adenoids. The London people put down their wine glasses and plates and began to move through the concourse. "Great show, Jack," said Preminger, helping himself to a final goat's cheese tartlet and a skewered Thai prawn. "And not a pie in sight!" "Thanks. Thanks for coming," said Jack. "Put that somewhere for me, will you," said Preminger, passing Jack his redundant cocktail stick before shaking hands and trotting off towards the coach. A proud and happy man, Jack asked his staff, all eight of them, to assemble in the cafeteria, and he thanked them for their effort. "Have all the Londoners gone?" he asked Maggie. "Yes," she said through her nose, peering out of the window as the back wheels of the bus rattled over the cattle grid. "Very good. So here's your reward," said Jack. He clapped his hands, and in through the double doors of the kitchen came Bernard, driving a forklift truck, and on it, the most enormous pie. A wild, ecstatic cheer reverberated among the tables and chairs. "Fill your wellies!" cried Jack. Tina from the gift shop could not restrain herself; she ripped off a section of the crust, dunked her arm in as far as her elbow, and smeared her face with rich brown gravy. Seth the gardener wasn't far behind, gnashing frenziedly at the crimped edging, followed by Millicent from publicity who hooked out a juicy piece of steak, went down on all fours and gorged on it like a starving dingo. Soon everyone was devouring the pie. Like all the great pies of history, the more they ate, the bigger it became. Jack threw his jacket into the corner of the room and whipped off his shirt and trousers. He was wearing blue swimming trunks. Standing on the rim of the metal dish he lowered himself through the light pastry topping. Maggie followed suit in her bra and pants, until all the staff of the Sculpture Farm were rolling or wading or lolling or lazing or helping themselves in the great slow pool of the pie. Now the forklift doubled as a diving board as Bernard belly-flopped from one of its prongs into the warm mush. It was only after retrieving a baby carrot from between his toes that Jack looked up and saw Preminger, who'd forgotten his wallet. "You people" he seethed. His face looked like the smell of a broken sewer in high summer.

Jack stood up. "I can explain everything," he said. A chunk of braised celery slithered over his sternum. Preminger hissed, "You told me the pie thing was over. Finished. You said it was safe in the north, Jack Singleton. But look at you. Call yourself a Sculpture Farmer? You couldn't clean out a hamster cage." "Forgive us," said Jack. "We're pie people. Our mothers and fathers were pie people, and their mothers and fathers before them. Pies are in our blood." "Don't tell it to me. Tell it to them," said Preminger, pointing to the window. On the other side of the glass stood the idling coach. Like a row of gargoyles, the faces of critics, sponsors, trustees, rich benefactors and famous names from the world of animal art looked out disgusted and appalled. Preminger swivelled on his heel and exited. The bus revved and departed. Leaving gravy footprints behind him, Jack wandered out of the building and into the landscape beyond. And the crocodile of staff followed, past the iron pigs, up to the granite bull on the hill, then along by the pit-pony carved in coal and the shimmering flock of stainless-steel geese in the far meadow. Finally they found themselves in a little temple in the woods, with tea-lights on the stone steps, the flames of which looked like the sails from a flotilla of tiny yachts in a distant bay. Torches to each corner of the building burnt and smouldered with an imperial pride. In front of Jack, soaked in pie juice, stood his loyal staff: Jethro with his three fingers; Maggie with her shopping problem; Tina who'd fallen in a quarry; Cormac who'd done time. Jack said, "In the horse I see the plough; in the bull I see the wheel; in the goat I see the scythe; in the pig I see the stove. Bernard," he shouted into the shadowy woods behind them, " bring out the custard."

Longside Gallery
Saturday 29 September 2007

Top right, Andy Goldsworthy, Hare blood and snow, 2004. Photo: courtesy John Jones.

Upon Unloading The Dishwasher

Even though Katy was desperate to end her affair with Raymond she agreed to a rendezvous at a local gallery to see the new Andy Goldsworthy exhibition. Standing in front of a canvas onto which the blood of a dead rabbit had dripped and congealed, Raymond said, "It's kind of rabbit-shaped – do you think that's the point?" When she didn't answer, Raymond raised his voice. "I SAID IT'S KIND OF RABBIT-SHAPED – DO YOU THINK THAT'S THE POINT?" When Katy finally replied, here's what she said. She said:

"Raymond, imagine my surprise when, upon unloading the dishwasher, I discovered the image of The World's Most Wanted Man imprinted on one of my best dinner plates. I phoned the Customer Service Hotline. This bored-sounding operative somewhere on the sub-continent said to me, 'So let me get this straight, madam, you've found The World's Most Wanted Man taking refuge in your dishwasher?' 'No,' I said, and explained again in plain English. He said, 'Mam, are you sure it isn't a gravy stain or the residue from a pork chop? Meat products can be very stubborn, and for heavy soiling we recommend a pre-soak. Also, you might want to try a longer cycle at a higher temperature, and can I ask which type of detergent you're using? Is it tablet or sachet?' Then maybe he heard my sobbing because he said, 'OK, we'll send somebody round.' Five minutes later there was a knock at the door and in came a policeman and priest. 'That's him all right,' said the officer, holding the dinner plate up to the light and confirming the identity of The World's Most Wanted Man. 'Is it a miracle?' I asked. The priest had closed his eyes and was sitting on the pedal-bin with his arms folded across his chest. The policeman laughed. 'Are you kidding – this is the ninth this week. And it isn't just plates. It's cups, dishes, ice cubes, toast, pizzas. A woman in Hull found him on the cheesy crust of a vegetarian lasagne.' Then he said, 'We'll have to take this appliance away, get the lab boys to give it the once-over.' Now I was crying again. I said, 'But it's Christmas Eve. I've got a party of twelve to cater for tomorrow, including Dr Roscoe and that poor boy who stands in the park all day flipping a coin. What shall I do?' He said, 'At times like this some people find that praying helps.' With his extendable baton he pointed at a place on the lino where I might kneel. I asked him if he'd join me, but he replied, 'I won't, if you don't mind. Like my old man told me, there's only two reasons for putting your hands together: one's for ironic applause, the other's to scrub up before dinner, and even then the palms don't actually touch because they're separated by an invisible and infinitely thin film of detergent. What you call soap.' "

Every word that Katy had uttered was complete cobblers. She knew it and Raymond knew it too. But the security guard had gone outside for a cigarette, and they were the only living souls left in the great, echoing hangar of the gallery. And Katy was aware with an absolute clarity of perception that the moment she stopped talking the fresh and bloody wound of Raymond's mouth would move quickly and incisively against her own.

God

Since I have made all things on water and land –
duke, emperor and king – with mine own hand,
to follow their inkling by sea or by sand,
so before my bidding every man should stand
with respect;
for giving life to this creature
by fairest of favour
man should love his creator,
by reason and repent.

I thought I showed man love when I made him to be
like all angels above, and of the trinity,
but now in great reproof full low lies he,
in league with sin on earth, and that displeases me
most of all.
Vengeance will I take
on earth for sin's sake
and with my fury will wake
both the great and small.

I regret nothing more than the day I made man.
Now he ignores his almighty sovereign.
I will scythe down therefore each beast, man and woman;
all have peril in store that unheeded my reign
and ill have done.
On earth, all rightness fails
and what thrives there is foul.
Of any with deserving souls
I find but one.

Henceforth shall I cut low this sinful crowd
with floods that shall flow and run hideously red,
and my cause is true, for no man fears my word.
As I say shall I do – with vengeance draw my sword
and bring a wet end
to all that bears life,
save Noah and his wife
who occasioned no strife
and did me not offend.

So to Noah my servant speedily will I go
not to drown but to save him and warn him of woe,
for on earth, sin rampaging now sweeps to and fro,
and men in wars waging, each the other's foe,
trade evil intent.
All shall I raze
with water and waves.
I will end their days
that will not repent.

Noah, my comrade, this command thee I tell:
a ship thou shall build of nail, board and keel.
In loyalty thy bond was truer than steel,
and my bidding you obeyed – so on earth shall thou feel
friendship's strength.
Of size thy ship shall lie
full thirty cubits high,
and fifty cubits wide,
and one hundred in length.

Anoint thy vessel with pitch and tar, without and within,
to keep sea-water far from seeping in;
and let no man it mar; and three cabins begin.
Use many a spar if the craft is to win
over water.
Make in this ark also
stalls down below
and pens in a row,
for beasts you must quarter.

One cubit in height a window shall thou make
and into the side one door shall create.
With thee shall no man fight, or my rage they provoke.
And when all is shipshape thy wife shall you take
onboard with thee,
and thy sons of good name:
Shem, Japheth and Ham
shall with you remain,
and their wives three.

For all shall be undone that live on earth's territory
by floods that from heaven shall fall aplenty.
It shall happen soon that it rains incessantly
and when seven days have done it shall endure for forty
without fail.
And take aboard next
two beasts of each sex,
no more and no less
before thou set sail.

And for thy survival when all this is wrought
stuff thy ship with victuals so to perish not;
As for beasts, fowl and cattle, keep them high in your thoughts,
for their sake I counsel that safety be sought
in great haste.
They must have corn and hay
and meat from day to day.

Now do thee as I say
in the name of the holy ghost.

The Song of Wandering Aengus

I went out to the hazel wood,
Because a fire was in my head,
And cut and peeled a hazel wand,
And hooked a berry to a thread;
And when white moths were on the wing,
And moth-like stars were flickering out,
I dropped the berry in a stream
And caught a little silver trout.

When I had laid it on the floor
I went to blow the fire aflame,
But something rustled on the floor,
And someone called me by my name:
It had become a glimmering girl
With apple blossom in her hair
Who called me by my name and ran
And faded through the brightening air.

Though I am old with wandering
Through hollow lands and hilly lands,
I will find out where she has gone,
And kiss her lips and take her hands;
And walk among long dappled grass,
And pluck till time and times are done
The silver apples of the moon,
The golden apples of the sun.

W. B. Yeats

Afterword
Clare Lilley, Head Curator

Yorkshire Sculpture Park shows work by modern and contemporary international artists, and creates projects with artists at all points of their careers. We work with sculptors, filmmakers, writers, performers, environmentalists and dancers, to name a few. It is fascinating to see how an artist, once asked to make a project, develops their ideas and ultimately executes them.

Simon Armitage has been associated with the Park for some years, and was invited to respond to the place and its people during our thirtieth year. He started in January 2007, still very much with the tenor and success of his much-lauded *Sir Gawain and the Green Knight* in mind; a book which was launched at YSP. This 14th century chivalric epic tale, bound to the seasons and seasonal change, was an initial preoccupation for Simon. Other ideas followed, including notions of making text-sculptures around themes such as memorial, light, and ephemerality. As Simon has explained, those concerns gradually changed until he found his true voice: that of words, of speech, of tonal resonance.

Bookended here with fitting poems by Frost and Yeats, the result of his year-long fellowship is this collection of writing: new poems that relate in very direct, and not so direct, ways to Yorkshire Sculpture Park and its machinations; together with texts which are translations from the Wakefield Mystery Plays. Also important – actually essential – were the readings themselves. Live performance is an essential part of Simon's work and at YSP each of the five readings was site-specific. They were given during a week in September at twilight, that liminal, shadowy time between day and night when the brain and body sense change. The accompanying CD reflects the tone of each of the readings, and the photographs here record how, until the last evening, small troops of people who had signed up for this experience, made their way across the landscape to various apposite outposts to hear Simon speak. The journeying to and fro, of strangers being brought together by a common interest, were as much a part of the experience as the readings themselves. Each was different, according to weather, the length of walk, the site of performance, the dynamics of disparate individuals knocking along together. Slicing through the everyday, illuminating thoughts and ideas with precision, is what Simon's texts achieved, is what this experiential process achieved. And a sort of magic was created by the whole.

There is a degree of magical realism inherent within the prose-poems; nothing too extreme, but a clear stretching of the here and now to encompass a world where desire and wanting make extraordinary things happen and where a kind of parallel universe can be glimpsed. So a long-lost child reaches out to her parents from a galaxy within their bedroom wall; instead of a dishwasher engineer, a woman is sent a priest and policeman; and the defiantly northern staff of a sculpture farm are found frenziedly eating and bathing in a massive, ever-expanding meat pie.

In these works references are made to YSP that are general and also specific, almost to the degree of being a skit: the ride-on lawnmower; the forklift truck; the skyspace aperture in the deer shelter; the tannoy system used at openings and the carefully observed hierarchy of food on offer; of YSP being a meeting place for lovers, both licit and illicit; and the cycles of growth and decay within the natural world.

By contrast, the Wakefield Mystery Plays are theatrical and characterful accounts of stories from the Bible, told by the common man as they were performed by the town's guilds and other associations, and handed down through written and aural tradition until they were recorded in their current form in the 15th century. At first sight, inclusion of Simon's translations of monologues from the Mystery Plays might seem a little anomalous, but they are carefully selected and they resonate with the places in which they were read. In the 18th century Camellia House, we heard the voices of Jesus' torturers – their casual brutality and earthy language chiming with their superstitious belief in the power of Jesus' clothes and interweaved with an understanding of the enormity of their actions. In the chilly, bucolic 19th century deer shelter, the shepherd declaims the social structure that keeps his class in its place, drawing connections between the mediaeval period, the 18th century when the Bretton Estate was principally designed, and contemporary Britain. In Andy Goldsworthy's clay-walled room in the Underground Gallery, cracked and pulsing, Lazarus spoke with a visceral, gutteral voice of the levelling of death: "both misters and masters from great heights | shall be brought under". From the Greek temple folly, hidden away beside the lake, and in a fine drizzle livid with dark light, came Joseph's lament – his confusion and anger of being wed to a maiden he must now believe is made pregnant by God. As in all of these excerpts, our (apparently) modern concerns are presented: "but this is how youth has always been | full of wanton ways". And finally, in the large open space of the Longside Gallery, to an audience of more than 200, God tells Noah that he is chosen to set the seed of all humanity. A story of creation, spoken in a room in which a powerful river form snakes across an entire glass wall; a room hung with the most basic of materials – dung, mud, blood – the raw stuff of life.

In the 18th and 19th centuries, the Wentworth and Beaumont families expanded and designed the Bretton Estate, setting it with architectural features and follies; baubles that they presumed would light their reputations and status. Over the last thirty years, YSP has worked to enable access – physical, emotional and intellectual – to this haven, surrounded as it is by a massive industrial and urban conurbation. In so doing, the Park has skewed and possibly upturned centuries of social division, enabling people from all walks of life to visit and to work here. The YSP staff comprises a miscellany of gardeners, educators, art historians, cooks, cleaners, carpenters, guards, artists, singers and players. Add to them the visitors, in all their rich diversity, and the artists, driven to push along unbeaten paths, and you have a fascinating melting pot.

This collection beautifully encapsulates that heady mix and expands way beyond the confines of the terrain. Simon's voice, his timbre, runs through and enlivens these words and it's hard to imagine the Second Torturer saying "bop him on the bonce" with anything other than a Marsden accent. Throughout this collection Simon points to the manifest failings of humankind – torturer, cheating lover, dispassionately unethical adolescent, the socially prejudiced, and those with unfounded superstition. And in exposing frailties, he also reveals what makes us so deliciously obtuse, vibrant and alive.

Acknowledgements
Peter Murray, Executive Director

Without the support of the Calouste Gulbenkian Foundation it would not have been possible to produce this book, which represents Simon Armitage's fellowship as Visiting Artist at Yorkshire Sculpture Park. I am most grateful for their generous support, which has enabled one of this country's most highly regarded artists to attempt new and innovative ways of working. Thanks must also go to Simon's publishers, Faber & Faber, for their assistance.

This publication has been developed from the limited edition booklet created for participants of the Twilight Readings, which Simon undertook in September 2007. Working alongside Simon, our Assistant Curator, Sarah Coulson, has designed a memorable book which, illustrated with stunning photographs by Jonty Wilde, captures a real sense of the atmosphere generated by the Readings. Both Sarah and Jonty deserve huge thanks for their impressive work.

A project like this takes a great deal of organising and planning, and requires the involvement of many from marketing, fundraising, security, information and catering. In particular, however, I want to thank Anthony Shepherd, who gave so much to the project and made the process so very enjoyable.

Clare Lilley, our Head Curator, has managed to co-ordinate this complex project and to create an opportunity for Simon to work at YSP. I am more than grateful to her for this and also for her perceptive Afterword.

Lastly, my personal and our collective thanks go to Simon Armitage, who has made a real impact on the YSP community and who has created a special project as part of our thirtieth year. This recent collaboration is, to an extent, a continuation of Simon Armitage's interest in YSP and it strengthens a relationship that we hope will continue to grow.

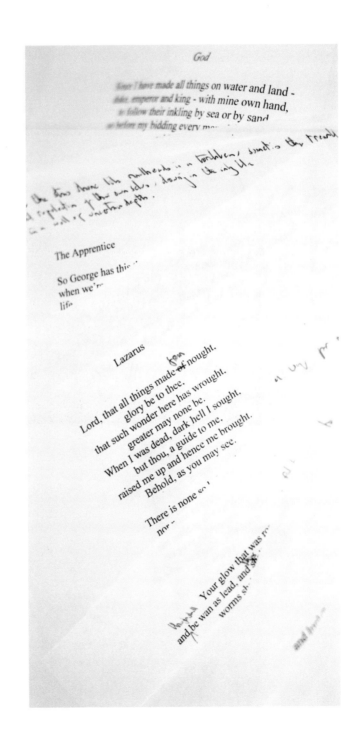

God

~~Since I have made~~ all things on water and land -
~~duke,~~ emperor and king - with mine own hand,
~~to follow~~ their inkling by sea or by sand
~~so~~ before my bidding every m⸺

The Apprentice

So George has this ⸺
when we'r⸺
lif⸺

Lazarus

Lord, that all things made ~~of~~ nought.
glory be to thee.
that such wonder here has wrought.
greater may none be.
When I was dead, dark hell I sought.
but thou, a guide to me.
raised me up and hence me brought.
Behold, as you may see.

There is none s⸺
nor ⸺

Your glow that was r⸺
and be wan as lead, and s⸺
worms sh⸺

in the global marke... details of my cam...
street, or scream the details of my ca...
hole of the cosmos hoping to bend the e...
I tell him I once swallowed a camellia ...
empty stomach, but he isn't listening a...
some chap who went at his camellia w...
shears. He's talking about such-and-s...
her camellia in front of the queen's carri...
which were beaten senseless by plain...
rendered down into potting compost...
set on fire on prime-time national t.v...
him that no matter how small and pi...
might seem to him, to me they ar...
with a wounding expression.
...eeing, all-knowing...
...ndisguis...

truly me thought it ragger
129: The play, in feyth, it was to rowme,
the play, in faith, which was going round
130: That he shuld, lay his hede downe,
that he should lay his head right down
131: And sone I bobyd hym on the crowne,
and then I bobbed him on his crown
132: That gam me thoght was good.
that game I thought was good
133: when we had played with hym oure fyll.
when we had played with him our fill
134: Then led we him vnto an hyll,
then led we him unto a hill
135: And ther we wroght with hym oure wil
and there we wrought him with our will
136: And hang hym on a rud,.
and hung him on a rood

lord how we cheered and laughed
and with a briar crowned that scruff
as though he were a king.
Then in due course
full curiously I thought
to wrap his corpse
in faith for him to swing.

But to my God I make a vow,
here have I brought this clothing now
to try the truth before your law
and in your sight.
Between me and my fellows two
these garments two of us must lose;
sir Pontius Pilate thou must choose,
this very night.

woe is him that never rests

this day or tomorrow.

But we (sely) shepherds that walk the moor

... out of the door

ld one get a ~~puffed~~ sleeve or a brooch nowadays
e care if you him grieve or dispute what he says
re no man deprive him of the power he ~~holds~~
nd yet no man believe one word that he says –

not one letter

He gets his ill-gains

with ~~boastful~~ braying claims

and brags ~~of being maintained~~

by men ~~even are greater~~

no wonder, as it stands, that we be poor,

for the tilth of our land lies fallow as the floor.

I tell you then:

we are fleeced and rammed,

with taxes slammed,

and tamed by hand

by these gentlemen.

·Thus rape us of rest — let Mary make them war

these pompous pests who make the plough tar

Some say it's for the best but we find contrar

thus are farm-hands oppressed: no hope do they

alive.

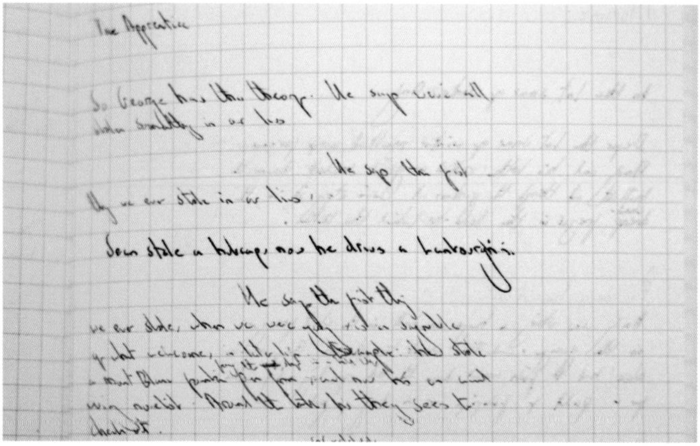

The Apprentice

So George has this theory. [illegible handwriting]

[illegible handwriting]

[illegible handwriting]

Sam stole a telescope, now he drives a lamborghini.

[illegible handwriting]

...it over fire of brushwood and
...the thinness of its flesh and the
... we bedded down in
...side of the hill. There was a
...here on our backs, it was as if
...ky blue eyeball of the sky,
...re the eyeball appeared to be
...George's theory, I said
...k you'll be, when you grow
... from somewhere in his
...sy voice he said, "I'm
... the hole in the roof
...verse itself, excessively
... rummaged about in
...natch, then said

...investment bankers and the stole
...ther's purse. Tod took a Curly Wurly
...hese. Claude says he never stole
... life, and he's an actor i.e. unemployed.
... a second, I stole a blue smurf dangling from a
... and Kirsty says, "So what more
...k." Every third Saturday in the
... from his mother's house and we
...e dog-track, sometimes into the
...k we headed into the Western
...der the stars and to get some
...r to son. With nothing more
...d thread of cotton we caught
...was all for tossing it back in
...e by slapping it down on a
... washing out its guts in the
... fire of brushwood and
...ess of its flesh and the

The Apprentice

George has this theory. He says we
all steal something whenever we grow, and
then part that we steal - that's what we
become." "I stole a pen out now I'm a
writer," he volunteers. We go around the
table, and it seems like the theory checks out.

Reynold's an investment banker
and he stole money from his mother's purse.
Chet said he never stole until he was top,
and his an interesting story between gifts.
Dennis up. "But how am I stole a finite chunk,
on a franchise, and Kelly says, "Exactly."
Either ... my business or embarrassment as
some stole one, and we ended with a pithy quote.
A couple of weeks later, don't it was then
too have how I took my son on a hunting
trip in the Sawy Mountains. We caught not

                                        Jet they incense?

the fish on the top of the
the fish on the top of the ... "Abandoned"
I said." What will you do when your son or you
up?" He was hijacked and then they up the
fell over.
          "You gotta be in execution," he
said Dennis.

              And then go to sleep

              Seeing them done every task
              or put this theon

Beneath the earth you ~~must~~ ... ...
... roof of your hall your ... ... mouth,
... the great sun small to you will ...
shall be your pall, and truth will ... ...

    Slime shall you wear,
     fiends will you fear,
    your flesh that was once fair
     shall ruefully rot.
    Instead of a stiff collar
tight bindings shall ~~wind~~ your throat.

I'll Be There To Love And Comfort You

The couple next door were testing the structural
fabric of the house with their high-pitched
[...] operatic [...] I said to Josie my eyes [...]
moment there was another [...] catch,
metallic and percussive [...]
[...] in the hidden [...] against the
tiled floor." Josie said." To [...] relax.
Take one of your [...] I breathless get up
[...] ten [...] we went to bed. With the
[...] out stepped my eyes into
the sandalwood. I was dreaming that there
[...] was laid on a [...]
cover with planet earth, then suddenly
felt some [...] through the window will
[...] above the [...]
[...] the moon. The only light is that of the new moon, even so,
I saw the cloudy [...] and colour, [...]
on the street [...] when [...] at that [...]
the full window. Josie [...] in [...] was
pushed till did it [...] on
sleep. She held the [...] head pulled free
[...] in a [...] across only
[...] to papers [...] I raised [...] the [...]
side will [...] across on the other
side will [...] the occasion [...] people or
some light. While there went, [...]
[...] electric [...] point [...]
[...] [...] something. I could not
[...] in there. The sun would [...]
above. When I had softly [...] the trembling [...]
[...] not of stew. There a [...] said, [...]
[...] Josie. Suddenly Josie— is she not to me.
She said," No babe. [...] I babe. Yes, Josie —
that's madness [...] all your."

~~Each was given a white-coloured wand~~
and had us bear it in our hand,
to offer with good intent.
Then all men held their wands up high,
but I was old and stood aside,
knowing not what they meant.

They lacked one. ~~All, they all did~~ chime.
Each and all, they
had offered wands, except for mine,
for I stood withdrawn.
Forward with wand they made me come,

Upon Unloading The Dishwasher

I imagine my surprise when you unload the dishwasher. I discovered the range of the World's Most Wanted Man invented in use of my best dinner plates. I phoned the Customer Service Hotline. The first and "Let's get this straight, sir — you pack the World's Most Wanted Man taking refuge in your dishwasher. No, I said to him, and explained to him a second time but I had already made perfectly clear. He said "Are you sure it isn't just a young stain in the residue from a fine soap." Heat products can be pretty stubborn, and especially a pre-soak, and also you might want to try a longer cycle at a higher temperature, and use too little amount of detergent you — is it a billet proof of such. Then he might have heard my anger because he said "Alright, well I'll send someone over." Five minutes later there was a knock at the door and a policeman and a nurse showed themselves in

Back in the ... ... as a ...
... buttons ... ...
parents of ...
for a man the ...
notice, let it ...
window of ...
fingerprints beg...
let one tell...
windows but g...
wall...
is slip on ...
and the sound ...
and the sound ...
... ...
and

So one day th...
coloured liver ...
... for the ...
the front ...
either put it ...
"Now make for ...
longer but ...
green, what's t...
let I want it ...
and get of the di...
the top, tablg...
... had be...
... of only side...

... ...
...

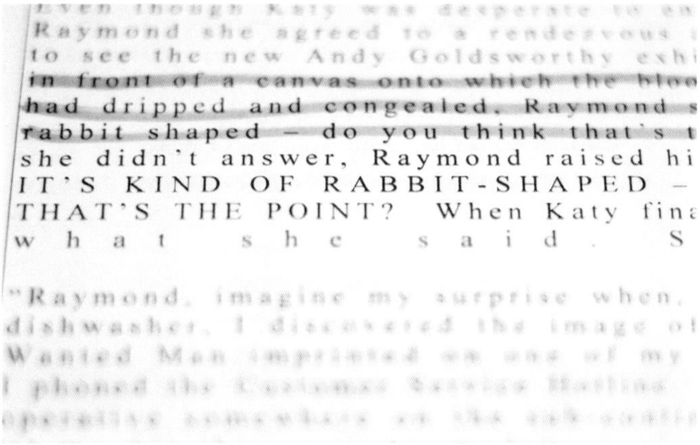

Even though Katy was desperate to av...
Raymond she agreed to a rendezvous ...
to see the new Andy Goldsworthy exhi...
in front of a canvas onto which the bloo...
had dripped and congealed. Raymond ...
rabbit shaped – do you think that's t...
she didn't answer, Raymond raised hi...
IT'S KIND OF RABBIT-SHAPED –
THAT'S THE POINT? When Katy fina...
what she said. S...

"Raymond, imagine my surprise when, ...
dishwasher, I discovered the image of ...
Wanted Man imprinted on one of my ...
I phoned the Customer Service Hotline ...
operative somewhere on the sub-conti...

Hypothetical — different significance

from Noah

God

Since I have made all thi
duke, emperor and kin
to follow their ink
so before my biddi

for givi

and being a wet end
to all that bears life
save Noah and his wife
who occasioned no strife
and did me not offend.

cow shit river

Audio CD listing:

Camellia House: Sunday 23 September 2007

1   My Camellias
2   *from* The Talents

Deer Shelter Skyspace: Tuesday 25 September 2007

3   The Apprentice
4   *from* The Second Shepherd's Play

Underground Gallery: Wednesday 26 September 2007

5   *from* Lazarus

Temple: Friday 28 September 2007

6   Robert Frost, *The Road Not Taken*
7   *from* The Annunciation

Longside Gallery: Saturday 29 September 2007

8   W.B. Yeats, *The Song of Wandering Aengus*
9   *from* Noah
10   The Practical Way to Heaven
11   I'll be There to Love and Comfort You
12   Evening